C000235847

# THE BRECON BEACONS

Tom Hutton

First published in Great Britain in 2009



Front cover: *Pen y Fan and Corn Du from Cribyn.*
Back cover: *River Usk near Llangynidr.*



British Library Cataloguing-in-Publication Data
A CIP record for this title is available from the British Library

ISBN 978 1 906887 02 5

**PiXZ Books**
Halsgrove House, Ryelands Industrial Estate,
Bagley Road, Wellington, Somerset TA21 9PZ
Tel: 01823 653777
Fax: 01823 216796
email: sales@halsgrove.com

An imprint of Halstar Ltd, part of the Halsgrove group of companies
Information on all Halsgrove titles is available at: www.halsgrove.com

Printed and bound by D'Auria Industrie Grafiche, Italy

# Contents

# Introduction

## The Area

The Brecon Beacons National Park is home to the most southerly mountains in Britain, and is understandably attractive to walkers of all types who flock to the area in their thousands. But there's more to this region than just towering peaks; and the valleys, rivers, lakes and moors provide perfect terrain for the walker that would prefer to keep his walking sociable and fun.

The national park covers over 500 square miles in total, and despite the name, it actually encompasses a number of different mountain ranges, or massifs, of which the Brecon Beacons are only one. The job of guarding the eastern edge of the park is shared between the beautiful Black Mountains that span the void between the Usk and Wye Valleys, and Abergavenny's three outlying peaks: Sugar Loaf, The Blorenge and Ysgyryd Fawr. The central ground is very much dominated by the distinctive outlines of the Brecon Beacons themselves, with the table top summit of Pen y Fan and its near neighbour Corn Du boasting the highest ground in all of Southern Britain. West of these iconic peaks, stands Fforest Fawr; a chain of windswept grassy ridges that carry fewer paths than the mountains that surround them, and are generally the domain of experienced hillwalkers with good navigation skills; West again lies the Black Mountain (singular); a lofty escarpment that towers over two concealed mountain lakes.

## The Walks

Gentle ground is hard to come by in such a mountainous area so some of the steeper, hillier walks are quite short, allowing plenty of time for rests along the way. Those that cross easier ground stretch to a few miles more, although not one is longer than 7 miles. They should all be achievable by families or groups of friends looking for a half-day excursion amongst stunning mountain scenery. (Sadly, none of the walks are toddler friendly so a back pack will be necessary). For ease of selection, the walks have been graded from one to three boots, where three is the toughest. It's recommended to start off with an easier route, just to gauge fitness and stamina. Where possible, the walks start at, or pass close to a pub or café; where lunch or a cuppa with big slice of cake, will provide a perfect excuse for a rest. But this is a fairly remote area, with few settlements let alone pubs, so where this hasn't been possible on the route itself, we've suggested the nearest suitable establishment for a spot of R&R after the walk's finished.

## Safety and comfort

As previously mentioned, this is a mountainous area and mountain weather can be both brutal and changeable, even in the middle of summer. Walking boots or stiff shoes are recommended for most of the walks, and it would be inadvisable to set off on any of the routes without at least a waterproof jacket. Take extra care on the outings that climb into the mountains, and perhaps carry a spare warm layer as well as some snacks and a drink, and even a pair of waterproof trousers. As a general rule though, avoid the higher-level walks when the weather's bad. Not only will it be unpleasant and perhaps dangerous to be up high in poor conditions, but it will also be difficult to navigate and it will defeat the object a little if you can't see the views when you do arrive at the top.

Whatever you do, don't rely on mobile phone reception when you're in the hills, it is patchy to say the least.

## Maps and navigation

All the routes follow public rights of way or cross land that the public has a right of passage across, and all were correct at the time of writing. Remember that conditions do change and routes do get diverted so consider this if the path on the ground seems to differ greatly from the description.

Starting points for each walk have been given with map references and postcodes – the latter to aid those using Sat Nav to get to the start. But once underway, walk descriptions have generally been given as right or left or straight ahead, with compass details in brackets purely to assist. These have been abbreviated as such: N (north), NNE (north-northeast), NE (northeast), ENE (east northeast) etc etc.

A sketch map is included with each walk description but these show only limited detail and won't be a lot of help if you do find yourself misplaced or want to lengthen or shorten the walk. It's advisable to carry a detailed map and a compass and even a GPS receiver if you have one. Two Ordnance Survey Maps cover the whole National Park: Explorer OL 12 (Brecon Beacons National Park West) & Explorer OL13 (Brecon Beacons National Park East). These are available in bookshops, Tourist Information Centres and even shops and garages.

For detailed availability, visit www.ordnancesurvey.co.uk/leisure.

# Key to Symbols Used

**Level of difficulty:**

Easy 🍀

Moderate 🍀🍀

More challenging 🍀🍀🍀

**Map symbols:**

- Park & start
- Tarred Road
- Unpaved road
- Footpath
- Building
- Church
- Triangulation pillar or other landmark
- WC
- Refreshments
- Pub

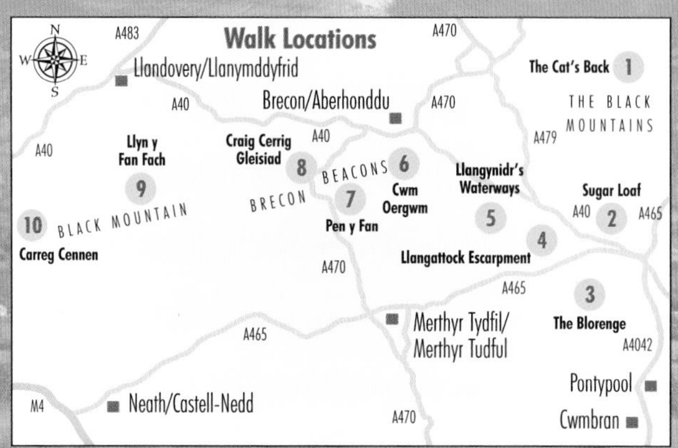

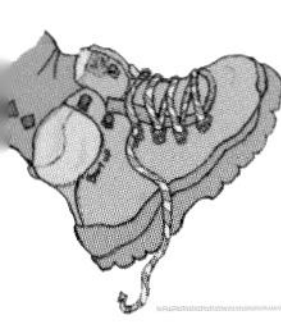

# 1 The Cat's Back

A brief sortie over the border into England provides scintillating walking along an airy ridge and a return via an attractive valley

**Level:** ♥♥
**Length:** 5 miles
**Terrain:** A clear path that runs along the crest of a narrow ridge, returning by a steep stony descent into a scenic valley. Some steep sections and a short walk along a quiet lane. Best saved for a good day.
**Park & Start:** Black Hill car park and picnic area, signposted at the head of a narrow lane easiest reached by driving north from the village of Pandy on the A465, north of Abergavenny.
**Start Ref:** SO288327 Postcode NP4 9SR
**Public Transport:** None
**Nearest Refreshments:** The Crown Inn at Longtown.

This walk is neither in the national park or even in Wales, yet, as you'll see within a few steps of starting out, the terrain and scenery dovetail wonderfully with the rest of the walks in the book, and the high car park and well-trodden path makes it possible to bring the typically more challenging ground of the Black Mountains within the grasp of the more casual walker. Even better, the simple linear format of the walk means that anybody finding the opening climb a bit on the tough side, can easily turn around and return directly to the car park, having still enjoyed the most spectacular section – the narrow, lofty ridge of Crib y Garth, usually known as the Cat's Back. Those making the full circuit will leave the ridge just after the highpoint of Black Hill, and descend into the Olchon Valley, via a steep rocky path that offers fine views as it drops to the fertile valley floor.

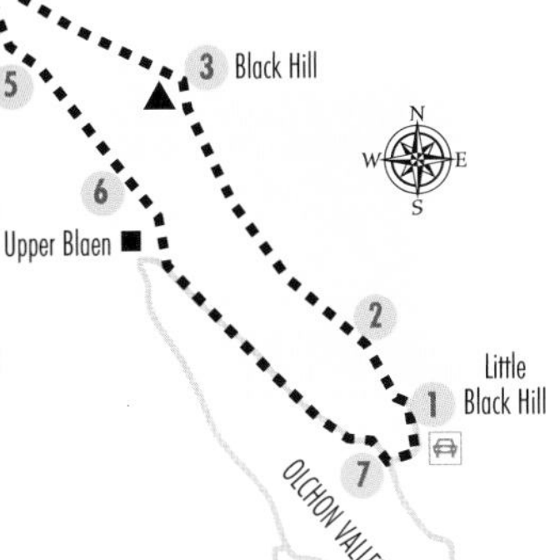

1 Start from the picnic area by heading up the hill and climbing over a stile (or nipping through the gate). You'll see a broad track (a public bridleway) veering right to contour around the hillside but you need to keep straight ahead (NW) to climb steeply up between gorse bushes onto the crest of the ridge.

2 After a tough start, the going eases and the ridge narrows sweetly to provide wonderful airy walking with stunning views west across the Black Mountains and east over the lowlands of Herefordshire and Worcestershire. Keep ahead (NW), all the time on the crest of the ridge, and apart from the odd rocky shelf, always easily negotiated to one side or the other, you'll have little to distract you for some distance. Eventually the narrow ridge broadens and you're faced with a short and easy climb on to Black Hill, the highest point of the walk.

*Wild Ponies on the Hatterrall Ridge.*

3 Enjoy the views, which include to the west, the Hatterall Ridge, the crest of which carries the England-Wales border, the National Park Boundary and the highest section of Offa's Dyke Path – a long distance footpath that is one of

*The Cat's Back.*

*Trig Point on Black Hill.*

*At 640m, Black Hill is actually the highest summit located totally in southern England. This is often over-looked, with the accolade usually being awarded either to High Willhays on Dartmoor, which weighs in at 621m or Kinder Scout, in Derbyshire's Peak District, which gets closer at 636m, although whether Derbyshire qualifies as southern England is another matter. The Hatterrall Ridge, which is visible from this walk, actually tops the 700m mark but as the border runs along the ridge, only half of the mountain lies in England.*

Wales's three National Trails. From the trig point, follow a faint path straight ahead (WNW) and pass close to a small pond. Continue for another half a mile and you'll see a small cairn on your left, marking a faint and narrow turn off.

4 Take the turning (SSE), which is vague to start with but quickly becomes a more defined path that leads easily between heather and bilberry. Continue towards the obvious notch in the hillside ahead, and on reaching this, you'll see the path drops steeply into the Olchon Valley beyond.

5 Drop down a series of rocky steps, stopping to enjoy the cascades on the Olchon Brook to your right. And then continue down onto easier ground, where the path cruises gently along, just a few metres above the river.

*Looking up at the Cat's Back.*

6 Cross a couple of small tributary brooks, that can be muddy, and continue to a gate in the corner. This leads onto a sunken track and this in turn, leads on to a narrow tarmac lane. Bear left onto the road and follow it easily down, along the valley floor, to a t-junction.

7 Turn left and follow the road uphill and around a sharp left hand bend to return to the car park.

*Top*
*The Cat's Back and the Olchon Valley.*

*Bottom*
*The Trig Point on Black Hill from one of the many small pools near the top.*

# 2 The Sugar Loaf

*A short but sharp mountain walk that leads onto one of the most distinctive summits in the whole National Park.*

**Level:** 

**Length:** 4 miles

**Terrain:** Clear paths over bracken-covered hillsides. Some steep sections and some places where navigation would be tricky in poor visibility. Best saved for a good day.

**Park & Start:** Mynydd Llanwenarth picnic area and car park, at the head of a narrow lane that leads off of the A40, a few miles west of Abergavenny.

**Start Ref:** SN268167 Postcode NP7 7ET

**Public Transport:** None

**Nearest Refreshments:** The Dragon's Head in nearby Llangenny.

Often the first mountain spied by visitors approaching the region, the distinctive conical outline of the Sugar Loaf, seems to be visible from almost anywhere in the surrounding area. At 596m (1,955ft) it's the tallest of the three Abergavenny Peaks, and it misses out on the celebrity status of 2,000ft (610m) – considered by many to be the qualification benchmark for a true mountain – by a measly 45ft (13m). It is nonetheless a wonderful hill to climb, firstly because its sloping western ridge gives a relatively easy and extremely scenic path to the summit, secondly because the rock-fringed, slender summit ridge really does have a 'big mountain' feel, and finally because it is so well-placed to offer views over the Black Mountains, Abergavenny and the Usk Valley. Even the summits of the central Beacons – Pen y Fan and Corn Du – are visible from the whitewashed trig point. This is definitely a walk to save for good weather.

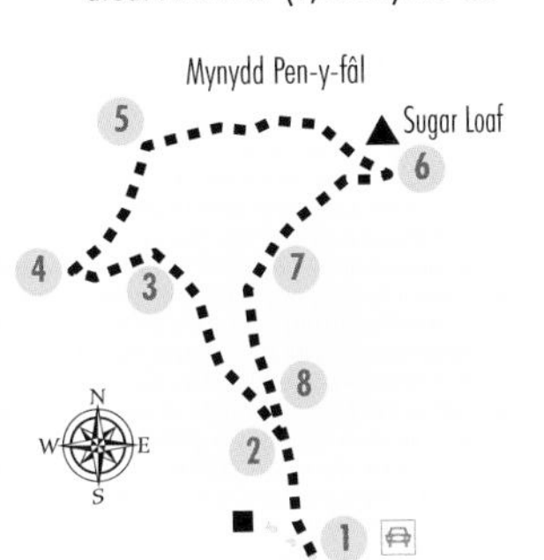

Sugar Loaf from Llangattock.

1 Start: The mountain isn't visible from the car park so start by looking directly up the steep slope above the car park (NE). There are three tracks leading away from the car park: a grassy one that leads past the National Trust sign to climb steeply up the hillside; a rougher grass and stone path that leads diagonally left from the top left hand corner of the car park; and a tarmac drive that leads left. You want the middle, half left one (NNW) that leads easily up to a corner of a dry stone wall.

2 There are many paths leading in all directions but most go the same way so don't worry too much. Keep straight ahead (NNW) with the wall to your left, and stay like this, ignoring any tracks to the right, and keeping the wall loosely to your left, until you are faced with a steep drop into a valley. Ahead now you can see the west ridge leading

Tree on Mynydd Llanwenarth, looking over the Usk valley

*Sugar Loaf from the south west. Brecon Beacons National Park.*

*Far-reaching views from Sugar Loaf summit.*

up to the summit. Drop into the valley, keeping the wood to your left, and at the bottom, you'll ford a small stream.

3 Now keep straight ahead (W) to climb steeply up a muddy path onto the shoulder of the ridge. You'll soon have a wall to your left and fine views back to Sugar Loaf over your right shoulder. Continue over a crest and then, with the corner of a wall and a gate directly head of you, turn right (NE) onto a rough path that leads towards the crest of the ridge.

4 After a few paces you'll pick up a clear grassy trail that leads through the gorse and bracken and onto a lovely airy crest with fine views over the valley beneath your feet and also west to the Black Mountains. Follow this, steeply at first, and then easily, and then steeply again to the western edge of the summit ridge.

5 Navigate around the rocky tip and continue easily (ESE) to the whitewashed trig point – a wonderful place to stop and catch your breath with fantastic views in all directions. It's also a great spot to survey the ground beneath your feet and to choose a descent route, as there are many paths running in all directions.

*Sugar Loaf's Welsh name is Mynydd Pen-y-fâl.*

*Sugar Loaf's summit.*

6 With the ridge you ascended to your right, you will see two major paths leading down from the summit and curving around the steep gash of the head of St Mary's Vale, which cuts into the slope below. From the trig point, walk ahead (S), to pick up the top of the main path and follow this steeply down.

7 As it levels it sweeps around the head of St Mary's Vale; and then it climbs slightly again with the crest of the hill to your right and the drop to St Mary's Vale to your left. Continue to a large grassy clearing, where two tracks meet, and turn right to cross the crest of the ridge, where you should be able to see a dry stone wall ahead.

8 At the wall, bear left, (SSE) and now keep it to your left, following a good track and retracing your earlier steps back towards the car park. The wall eventually dips to the right but you should keep straight ahead for a few more minutes to drop to the car.

*Blackthorn bushes on Mynydd Llanwenarth.*

*The slopes of Sugar Loaf are home to many small birds including meadow pipits and skylarks, and ravens are often seen on the summit, riding the updrafts. In winter, the heathery sections shelter a few hardy red grouse.*

# 3 The Blorenge

*A winding route across a gentle giant of a mountain high above the streets of Abergavenny.*

**Level:** 

**Length:** 6 miles

**Terrain:** Easy to follow footpaths over a high mountain. Some places can be muddy and navigation would be difficult in poor visibility.

**Park & Start:** Keeper's Pond car park, just off the B4246, halfway between Llanfoist and Blaenavon.

**Start Ref:** SO254107 Postcode NP4 9SR

**Public Transport:** None

**Nearest Refreshments:** The Cordell Country Inn is close to the start.

At 559m, the Blorenge towers above Abergavenny and the Usk Valley, marking the boundary of the National Park and providing an imposing natural divide between the mainly agricultural Monmouthshire hills and the once industrial valleys of South Wales. It's a wonderful mountain in a fascinating location that provides far-reaching views as well as plenty of evidence of the region's industrial past. The walk starts high, right on the cusp of the two contrasting landscapes, but then gradually drops towards the Usk, offering great views across the river as it goes. After a visit to a wonderfully-situated nature reserve, it climbs back up, passing the summit and a touching monument before finishing easily. The area was immortalised by Alexander Cordell's *The Rape of the Fair Country,* and an inn bearing his name is well-situated just down the hill from the start and finish.

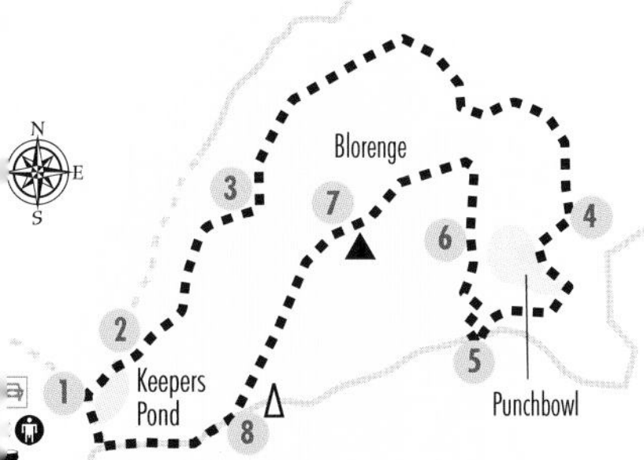

1 Start by walking to the interpretation board and looking at this with the pond beyond. Turn left to walk to the pond's southern tip, where you'll find a clear, wheelchair friendly path that rounds the tip of the pond and carries on along the shore, with the pond to the right. Continue to the far end where you'll cross a footbridge.

2 Now bear right (NE) on to a clear grassy path and follow this easily along with the main ridge up to the right. The path gradually veers around to the right to reveal great views over the Usk Valley and Abergavenny. Stay with it, at one stage going through a stony cutting, until you reach a cairn and marker post, with a narrow trail dropping to the left.

*The interpretatian board at Keeper's Pond.*

3 Take this and follow it steeply down (N) until it eventually joins a broader, clearer track above a wood. Turn right (ENE) onto this and ignore footpath off to the left to carry on along the clear track, which is actually an old tram road known as Hill's Tram road after the Blaenavon Iron Master, Thomas Hill. Follow this easily around the foot of the hillside, eventually passing a tunnel to your right. Stay with the track, which runs around the hillside neither climbing nor dropping, until you reach a gate at the entrance to the Punchbowl Nature Reserve.

4 Keep ahead again (S) and after a few more minutes' walking you'll come to the pond at the heart of the Punchbowl. Keep the water

*A wooly welcome.*

to your right and continue ahead, soon climbing steeply on a rough rooty track. Keep ahead to a gate and go through this to continue to a road.

Turn right onto the road, and after passing the end of the wood on the right, turn right again (NNW), onto a narrow path, signed Iron Mountain Walk. Follow this upwards, with the wall to your right, and now stay with the main path as it climbs away from the wall, then back close to it, then away from it for a last time. Continue upwards until you join a clear sunken track.

6 Turn right onto this and follow it up between piles of spoil, until you reach a hut. Turn left (WSW) to keep the hut to your right, and climb steeply for a short distance before continuing easily along a peaty path. Stay with this to the summit, which is marked with a trig point concealed in the rocks.

7 From the summit, keep ahead to follow a continuation path towards the two masts. As you approach the masts, you'll see a car park beneath it. Continue into the car park, where a sharp right turn (N), beyond an interpretation board, leads to Foxhunter's Grave.

*The Blorenge from Foxhunter car park.*

*The Blorenge.*

*A sea of cloud on the flanks of the Blorenge.*

*Foxhunter was a show jumping horse who, ridden by Welshman, Sir Harry Llewellyn, won Britain's only gold medal in the 1952 Olympic Games, in Helsinki. They won 78 international trophies together during the fifties, and when Foxhunter died in 1959, he was buried on top of the Blorenge. Sir Harry, who lived near Abergavenny, died in 1999 and his ashes were scattered close to the resting place of his beloved horse.*

*Foxhunter's Grave.*

**8** Return to the car park and carry on out onto the road. Turn right (SW) and follow the road for around half a mile to a junction with the B4246. Turn right to return to the Keeper's Pond car park.

*Walkers at Keeper's Pond.*

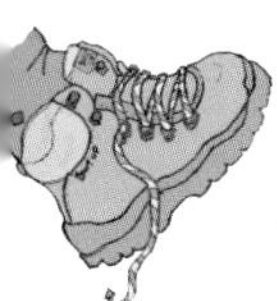

# 4 Llangattock Escarpment

*Easy going but with huge views; this is one of those walks that seems to give more than it takes.*

The views across the Usk Valley from the Llangattock escarpment have got to be some of the finest in the whole national park, but even these are challenged by the vista of the limestone cliffs of Craig y Cilau lit up by the early morning sun – especially in autumn when the trees add a warm, russet hue to the scene. The walk starts high, and apart from one short, steep descent, and an equally short but steep ascent, is mainly on the flat. But amongst scenery this special, it feels like a mountain walk, and the same precautions should be taken as for the tougher walks in the book. It's an isolated spot so there are no refreshments at hand, but Crickhowell and its pubs and cafés are just a short distance away, and the perfect place to end the day.

5
4
3
2
7
8
6
9
1
Caves
Cliffs
Pant-y-rhiw
Lime Kiln
Cliffs
N
W
E
S

**Level:**

**Length:** 5 miles

**Terrain:** Mainly clear paths around a steep hillside. One short, steep descent and one short, steep climb. The tracks can be confusing, although it would be difficult to get lost, so a good day is best for navigation and views.

**Park & Start:** Llangattock parking area: just off the minor road that runs between Bryn Mawr and Llangattock village.

**Start Ref:** SO209153 Postcode NP8 1LG

**Public Transport:** None

**Nearest Refreshments:** The Vine Tree in Llangattock village.

*The Lonely Shepherd guards the east end of the escarpment.*

**1** Start by walking back down the access track to the road and turning left (NW). Follow this to a sharp right hand bend and keep straight ahead (NW) to follow a broad track past some cottages on the left and then one (Pant y Rhiw) on the right. Carry on beyond a barrier and onto open hillside and keep going until you see a couple of grass-covered piles of spoil on the right and some large boulders ahead.

**2** The track narrows now and a quick search to the right of the boulders will reveal a steep path dropping straight down the hillside – a telltale sign of an old quarrying incline. Take this path and continue carefully down to the corner of the wood below, where you'll see the remains of an old wheel-man's hut and also a bench, with great views.

*Looking across the Usk Valley – Pen Cerrig-calch from Mynydd Llangattock.*

**3** Turn left (W) onto a narrow but clear path that can be covered by bracken in the summer and follow it uphill for a few paces and then level around the hillside, with great views ahead to the imposing cliffs of Craig y Cilau. It eventually drops to the floor of the valley where you'll meet a wall and a stream.

*The steep slopes of Craig y Cilau.*

4 Turn left, with the wall to your right, to walk along a rough, often rocky path that climbs steadily around the foot of the hill-side. Continue for nearly a mile, passing the Nature Reserve boundary, and then, still on the obvious path, divert left slightly, to cut across between two wall corners. At the far corner, look left for a faint narrow path that cuts back very sharply to start up the steep hillside. There is actually a small marker post on the left but this is often covered by bracken. This is the main uphill section of the walk.

5 Follow the path, which is rough but mainly level to start with, and stay with it as it steep-ens to climb to a marker post – a

*Spoil heaps from the quarries of the Llangattock escarpment.*

*Imposing limestone cliffs in Pinnacle Bay.*

Looking east along the spoil heaps.

sure sign you're in the right place. Keep ahead for another few paces and you'll eventually reach a good level track – an old tram road.

**6** Turn right for 300m to the locked entrance to Ogof Agen Allwedd, the entrance to one of the longest cave systems in Britain. Then

Eglwys Faen Cave.

*The caves to your right are known as Eglwys Faen, which translates to Rock Church. It is possible to climb a short zigzag path on the right of the caves to the largest entrance. A torch might be useful and the rock can be slippery.*

return to this junction and continue along the level path, passing a cluster of caves on your right.

7 Shortly after the caves, you'll pass a nature reserve board and a few hundred metres further on again, you'll see a narrow path forking off to the right. Take this and climb steeply up onto a grassy plateau, covered with boulders and small piles of spoil.

8 With the cliffs always to your right, follow the narrow path as it undulates along, keeping right at any forks you meet. You'll eventually meet a clearer broader track that heads leftwards around some huge banks of spoil at Chwar Pant-y-Rhiw.

9 Continue along this until a good track joins from the right, this comes through the cutting between the banks and the quarry faces. At the next fork, by a concrete bunker, keep left (SE) and follow the track along to a junction of tracks by a ruined lime kiln. Turn half left (E) to stay on the main track and follow it back down to the car park.

*Ruined lime kiln on the Llangattock escarpment.*

*This area bristles with industrial history. The limestone escarpment was quarried from the early 19th-century, if not earlier, and the tracks that the walk follows were once all part of the sophisticated transport network used to get the quarried stone and lime down to the Brecon & Monmouthshire Canal, near Llangattock village.*

# 5 Llangynidr's Waterways

A moderate waterside walk that follows the River Usk on the outward leg and the Monmouthshire and Brecon Canal on the way back.

**Level:** ♥ ♥
**Length:** 4 miles
**Terrain:** A mix of rough riverside trails and easy canal towpath, with a couple of short sections on quiet lanes.
**Park & Start:** Llangynidr village car park, on the B4558, halfway between Crickhowell and Talybont on Usk.
**Start Ref:** SO155195 Postcode NP8 1NJ
**Public Transport:** Good
**Nearest Refreshments:** The Coach and Horses at Llangynidr is on the walk.

The Monmouthshire and Brecon Canal follows the line of the sylvan River Usk from Brecon to the old docks at Newport. In places the river and the canal keep themselves to themselves, spreading out across the valley floor, but in others they get very close, with the canal actually crossing the river near Llanfrynach. This walk explores a beautiful section where the canal and river form a logical loop, close to the village of Llangynidr.

The outward leg, which follows the banks of the river very closely, is rough in places, and the rocks can be slippery too. But it's always good to get the hardest bit out of the way early, especially as there's a good refreshment stop in Llangynidr. The canal towpath offers an easy and scenic stroll to the finish.

N
E
S
River Usk
4
3
5
6
Canal
2
River Usk
Llangynidr
Canal
1

*Cascades on the River Usk near Llangynidr.*

1 Start by walking out of the small gate in the corner of the car park and turn right onto the B4558 for just a few paces. Cross the road and turn left into Cyffredyn Lane, which you now follow easily down, over a bridge over the canal, where you pass your return route. Continue until you round a sharp right hand bend and then turn left onto a walled footpath that leads down to the banks of the River Usk.

2 Turn left upon reaching the river, and follow the path – sandy in some places, rocky in others – to a stile. Keep ahead across a meadow and keep aiming in the same direction to cross a series of stiles, always with the river down to your right. One or two of the rocky

*Llangynidr Bridge was originally constructed in the late 16th-century and would have carried packhorses, hence its narrow width. Looking west from it, you can see the obvious rounded hill of Tor y Foel as well as the foothills of the central Brecon Beacons.*

*The sixteenth-century Llangynidr Bridge.*

*Coach and Horses in Llangynidr.*

sections can be very slippery when wet. After half a mile or so, you'll come to a bench which offers good views over a lovely cascade.

**3** Keep ahead from here and eventually you'll reach a tarmac drive, with a gate ahead marked Pen Isha Coed. Don't go through but instead turn right and then straight away right again onto a narrow path. Now trend leftwards to follow the narrow footpath alongside a fence with bushes between you and the river. Stay with the path now until you reach the road at the lovely old Llangynidr Bridge.

Cross the road and follow the continuation of the footpath

*Lock on the Brecon and Monmouthshire Canal near Llangynidr.*

*River Usk and Tor y Foel from Llangynidr Bridge.*

as it runs along the edge of a series of gardens before dropping once more to the banks of the river. Continue upstream, first in woodland and then in the open with fine views. Ignore a footpath to the left and continue to a set of steps that lead you away from the river.

5 Turn right at the top and follow the drive up to a road. Turn right onto this and follow it alongside the canal, above one of Llangynidr's five locks. Follow the road to a junction by the Coach and Horses – a fine place to quench thirst or perhaps a bite of lunch before continuing.

Retrace your steps back to the canal towpath by the lock, and now follow this easily eastwards. You'll pass beneath two bridges and then leave the canal by a stile on the left just before you duck under a third. You are now on Cyffredyn Lane, the lane you followed at the start. Turn right to retrace your earlier steps back to the village and car park.

*The Monmouthshire and Brecon Canal, originally known as the Brecknock and Abergavenny Canal, was built between 1797 and 1812 to transport stone and lime from the area's many quarries. Although it threads its way through some very mountainous terrain, over 23 miles (36.8km) of its total 33 miles (53km) are completely flat – a remarkable engineering achievement. The canal drifted into disrepair after the quarrying stopped in the early 1900s, but it has since been completely restored by the British Waterways Board with support from the National Park and it was reopened for leisure use in 1970.*

*Originally part of the Manor of Tretower, Llangynidr village is now home to around 1000 people. It sits at the foot of Mynydd Llangynidr – a huge swathe of austere moorland that is peppered with caves and pot holes.*

# 6 Cwm Oergwm

*A lovely walk that focuses on a stunning valley rather than the summits that tower above it.*

**Level:**
**Length:** 6.5 miles
**Terrain:** Mainly clear paths in woodland and across open moorland in a valley, where the weather wouldn't be too much of an issue. Note that the crossing of the Nant Mengasin would be awkward after heavy rain. If in doubt, continue upstream until it becomes easier.
**Start:** Llanfrynach
**Start Ref:** SO074257 Postcode LD3 7AZ
**Public Transport:** Good
**Nearest Refreshments:** The White Swan in Llanfrynach is near the start.

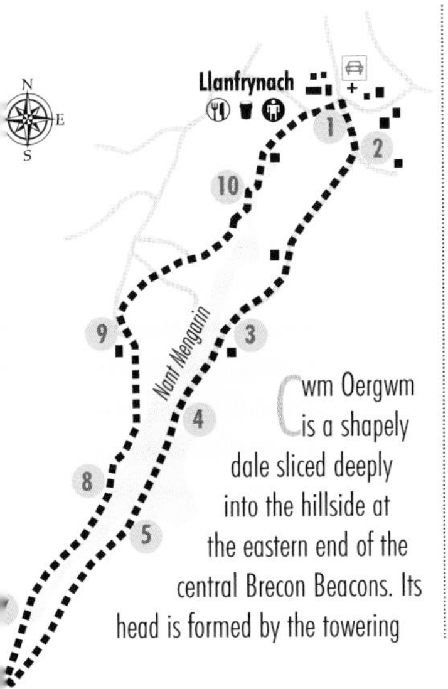


Cwm Oergwm is a shapely dale sliced deeply into the hillside at the eastern end of the central Brecon Beacons. Its head is formed by the towering cliffs of Craig Cwmoergwm and Craig Cwareli, and the ridge that crowns them is slung loosely between the rounded summits of Waun Rydd and Fan y Bîg. Just two valleys to the west stands the highest of all the Beacon peaks, Pen y Fan, which is explored by walk 7.

This walk explores the lower reaches of Cwm Oergwm, starting from the small village of Llanfrynach which has both public transport connections and a lovely pub. After climbing easily through woodland, it emerges onto open moorland, where it continues upwards to ford the stream beneath towering peaks. The return also follows woodland to start with but this gives way to easy footpaths across sheep pasture and it finishes sweetly with a lovely riverside section.

1 Set off with the public toilets to your right and the church to your left. Walk along the road for a few paces and turn right (SW) by the telephone box, with the White Swan down to your left.

2 Follow this lane down over a bridge and then turn first right, up the narrow Tregaer Road. Follow this easily upwards for just over 1 mile, passing farm buildings at Caerau, and later a remote house, where the tarmac ends and the road becomes a stony, dusty track.

3 Keep heading up the track and ignore a left turn to go through a waymarked gate into forestry. Cross a stream after half a mile and then keep ahead through a gate that leads out onto National Trust ground.

4 The path is difficult to discern in places here but keep heading up the valley, with the Nant Mengasin down to your right and you can't really go wrong. Go through another gate, and ford another stream, and shortly after this, you'll come to yet another gate that leads out onto open moorland, with Fan y Bîg towering above you at the head of the valley.

5 Stay with the rough path, with a tumbledown wall to your right, and when the wall peels away right, to drop to the Nant Mengasin, bear right onto an obvious path to follow it down. Note the huge boulder to your left.

6 Cross the stream at the obvious ford, where you'll see a lovely succession of waterfalls tumbling down the hillside above you. If the stream is in spate, it may be easier to cross above the waterfalls, but if the levels are too high, it may be better to return the way you came. A rough path leads up the other bank and follow this for around

Cascades in Cwm Oergwm.

100yds, keeping a careful eye open for a faint path forking off to the right (NNE).

7 Take this, and follow it around the hillside, neither climbing nor dropping. This leads to a gate, signed with a bridleway arrow, which you should go through to continue in the same direction. Keep ahead when a track forks left, and keep the fence on your right the whole time until you see a bridleway waymarker on a tree stump on the left.

8 Turn left here and follow further markers to stay on the main track until the track swings left by a metal farm gate, to go through a bridlegate and climb slightly with a wall to the right and a fence above on the left. This becomes a sunken track that leads to a gate where the bridleway has been diverted. Bear right into the field, and then turn left to continue parallel to the original track. This leads beneath holiday cottages to a lane.

9 Turn right, and then, after 300yds, turn right, through a waymarked gate, onto a footpath. Take this diagonally left across the field to a stile in the corner, and then keep the hedge to your right to drop to another lane. Cross this and go through the gate ahead to drop straight down the field edge to another gate. Go through this to another, and then bear slightly right to drop to a series of waymark posts that lead along the banks of a stream.

10 Bear right as directed to another post that sends you left, through a gate and over a brook. Now follow the obvious path ahead, with the Nant Mengasin down to your right. This leads out into sheep pastures, and if you continue in the same direction you'll soon reach a gate that leads onto a narrow lane. Turn right onto this and then turn right again to return to Llanfrynach.

# 7 Pen y Fan

The toughest walk in the book but worth the toil for the wonderful far-reaching views from the highest mountain in Southern Britain.

Celebrated as the highest mountain in both the National Park and the whole of Southern Britain, Pen y Fan is naturally a very popular mountain to climb. Despite its lofty height – the top stands 886m (2,700ft) above sea level – it's flat-topped summit is within reach of most averagely fit walkers providing they choose a good day to do it and, of course, they take their time on the long, steady climb over its steep slopes. The climb starts from the highest of the nearby car parks, minimising the amount of uphill needed, and it follows good paths throughout, meaning there are unlikely to be any navigation worries. That said, it's the toughest walk in this book so it's worth building up a bit of walking fitness with some of the other walks before setting off. A good day will also make it more comfortable and provide better views.

**Level:** 🥾🥾🥾
**Length:** 5 miles
**Terrain:** Clear paths over bracken-covered and grassy hillsides. Some steep sections and the odd boggy patch. Best saved for clear weather.
**Park & Start:** Storey Arms car park on the south side of the A470, between Merthyr Tydfil and Brecon.
**Start Ref:** SN982203 Postcode LD3 8NL
**Public Transport:** Good
**Nearest Refreshments:** Apart from snack vans in both car parks, the Tai'r Bull at Libanus isn't far away.

*Pen y Fan in full winter clothing from Cwm Sere.*

1 Start: Cross the road and hop over the stile, next to the telephone box, outside the Storey Arms Outdoor Adventure Centre. This leads onto a clear but rough path that climbs up alongside a plantation. Continue beyond the top of this and over open moorland, with a bare rounded summit to your left. You'll shortly arrive at a stile.

2 Cross this and keep straight ahead (E) to dip into a valley that carries the infant Afon Taf Fechan – eventually to become the Taff River that empties into the sea at Cardiff, a few miles south of here. Keep straight ahead (E) to climb steeply away from the stream on a badly eroded track. Stay with this until it until it reaches an escarpment edge, high above the deep valley of Cwm Llwch.

3 Below you now you'll see a small mountain lake – Llyn y Cwm Llwch – and dropping steeply to this are the precipitous northern slopes of Corn Du. But before heading for this, bear left (NW) and follow the path down for 300 metres to the Tommy Jones Memorial (you will need to climb back up from this so only go if you feel you've got the energy).

*Pen y Fan and Corn Du tower above Llyn y Cwm Llwch.*

Pen y Fan and Corn Du from Cribyn.

*The infant Afon Taf Fawr and Corn Du.*

**4** From the memorial, which is a truly touching spot, head back to the point where you joined the escarpment and then continue along it, with the steep drop to your left, to continue up towards Corn Du. The summit is crowned with a sprawling cairn.

**5** The way to Pen y Fan is straightforward now. Cross Corn Du (E) and drop easily into a shallow saddle that separates the two peaks. From here, keep ahead (ENE) to scale the short slope that leads to the top. The summit itself is flat but the north and northeast faces are incredibly steep and should be viewed with great care.

**6** To descend, walk back across towards Corn Du and then bear left to follow the obvious track that contours around the mountain into a pass known as Bwlch Duwynt. Here keep pretty much straight ahead (SW), with the summit up to your right, and a clear path leading south onto the ridge of Graig Gwaun Taf. If you're in any doubt, the path you want is the most prominent, built from stone in places, and it heads downhill, whereas the others climb slightly first.

*The north east face of Pen y Fan.*

**7** Follow the track easily down for just over a mile and you'll see the Taf Fawr River down to your right. As you near the bottom, this is jewelled with some fine cascades that are worth a visit.

**8** Eventually you'll reach a bridge over the Afon Taf Fechan. Cross this and continue into the large car park beyond. Now turn right (NNW) to walk to the far end of the car park where a path leads through trees to the A470. Stay on this side, with the plantation to your right, until you can cross safely back to the place where you started.

*Tommy Jones was a 5-year old boy who visited the area with his father, a coalminer, in August 1900 to see his grandfather, who lived in a farm north of the mountains. He left his father with some soldiers and followed his 13-year old cousin, Willie, to his grandmother's house. Tragically, the two boys became separated and Tommy, who was trying to return to his father, got lost. After a huge search, which lasted weeks, his body was discovered on September 2nd, high on the mountainside near to where the obelisk stands now. He'd died of exhaustion and exposure. The story is a chilling reminder of what savage places mountains can be.*

*Cribyn from Pen y Fan.*

# 8 Craig Cerrig-gleisiad

An easy stroll into the heart of a nature reserve followed by a steep but short sortie onto one of the more accessible tops of Fforest Fawr.

The pathless, windswept, grassy ridges of Fforest Fawr are on the whole, the domain of the experienced walker and navigator, but there are a few places where good paths penetrate the wilderness and this walk exploits one of them: the spectacular National Nature Reserve of Craig Cerrig-gleisiad. This is a fascinating place to explore with dark and brooding cliffs towering over rough, heather-covered hillsides. The north-facing cliffs were scooped out of the hillside by the retreating glaciers of the last ice age, and the cool, shady aspect of the cliffs, coupled with the altitude – the car park sits some 340m (1,115ft) above sea level – have created perfect conditions for rare arctic-alpine plants to continue to flourish here.

Above the cliffs, the summit of Fan Frynach gives a taster of the walking in this part of the National Park, but like many of the mountain walks in this books, it shouldn't be attempted in poor visibility, where route finding would be very difficult.

**Level:**

**Length:** 4 miles

**Terrain:** Clear paths over bracken and heather-covered hillsides with one or two very boggy stretches – boots recommended. There are a couple of steep sections and navigation near the summit of Fan Frynach might be difficult in poor visibility.

**Park & Start:** A lay-by or pull-in on the west side of the A470, a few miles south of Libanus. Storey Arms car park on the south side of the A470, between Merthyr Tydfil and Brecon.

**Start Ref:** SN971222 Postcode LD3 8NH

**Public Transport:** Good

**Nearest Refreshments:** The Tai'r Bull at Libanus isn't far away.

*Craig Cerrig-gleisiad in winter.*

**1** Start by going through the kissing gate at the back at of the lay-by and follow the clear, level footpath up the valley, with a stream to your left, for 300 yards to a dry stone wall. (To shorten the walk, continue ahead here to explore the nature reserve beneath the cliffs and then return via the same path).

**2** Go through the gap in the wall and turn right (NNW) to follow the clear path around the hillside with the wall, which is a fine example of a renovated dry stone wall to your right. Drop to cross two brooks, both times climbing back out of the steep sided gullies that they run in, and then continue, on a path that can be very boggy, until you finally reach a stile that leads onto a clear track, with fine views to the north.

**3** Turn left (SW) onto the track and climb steeply up the hill, now with great views east to Pen y Fan and Corn Du – the highest mountains in the park and the subject of walk 7. Eventually you'll come to a gate and a stile that give access to open moorland beyond. Continue along the track until a clear turning to the right leads you to the trig point that marks the summit of Fan Frynach. (In poor visibility, it would

*Looking up at the cliffs of Craig Cerrig-gleisiad.*

Craig Cerrig-gleisiad.

be a safer bet to ignore this part of the walk and continue on the main path, with the fence to your left, until you reach point 5).

4 From the trig point, face back the way you came and you'll see two tracks leading away from the trig point. Take the right-hand one (SE) and ignore a fork to the right almost immediately. Continue to another fork and bear right to drop back onto the main track. Turn right onto this (S) and follow the fence along until you spot a stile on your left.

5 Cross this (waymarked Beacons Way) and follow the path slightly leftwards (NE) across the hillside, ignoring a right fork, until you reach a junction with another path in an obvious shallow groove. Bear right here to follow a line of fence posts steeply down to a grassy bank of glacial moraine.

*Frozen waterfalls near Craig Cerrig-gleisiad.*

*The north-facing cliffs of Craig Cerrig-gleisiad – which translates to Blue-stone Rock – were formed by glacial action during the last ice age. The ice scoured out the deep hollow in the hillside that we see today, before depositing the rocks it picked up into large banks known as moraine. As well as the alpine-arctic plants mentioned above, the nature reserve is home to 16 different species of butterfly and over 80 species of bird.*

6 You are now in the heart of the reserve and should take a few minutes to explore before heading

back to the car. From the moraine, bear around to the left to follow the path around other banks and eventually down to the stream that you followed on the way in.

7 Keep ahead now, with the stream to your right, and you'll shortly come to the gap in the wall and the path you followed earlier that will lead you back to the car park.

*Steep cliffs of Craig Cerrig-gleisiad.*

# 9 Llyn y Fan Fach

An easy linear walk that leads to a magnificent lakeside picnic spot at the foot of some of the region's most spectacular mountains.

**Level:**
**Length:** 2.5 miles
**Terrain:** A clear and wide but rough, stony track that leads to a delightful lake shore deep in the heart of the mountains.
**Park & Start:** A small car park at the end of a very small and rough lane, a few miles south east of Llanddeusant. The village is approximately 10 miles south of Llandovery, just off the A4069 at Pont-ar-Lechau.
**Start Ref:** SN798238 Postcode SA19 9UN
**Public Transport:** None
**Nearest Refreshments:** The Cross Inn at Llanddeusant isn't far away from the start.

Unlike the rest of the walks in this book, which are circular, this outing is essentially a there and back type route – although there is an option for a loop around the lake once it's reached. But it earns its inclusion for offering easy, relatively family-friendly access to some spectacular mountain scenery that would otherwise be the exclusive domain of the more experienced walker. The key is an old water company road that leads from the remote hamlet of Llanddeusant to the glistening waters of Llyn y Fan Fach, sometimes also known as the 'magic lake' for the part it plays in a local legend.

The track is rough and stony in places, but it's easy to follow, never too steep, and it's also fairly short, meaning even the slowest party could be unwrapping their sandwiches on the lake's shore within an hour of leaving the car park, with most visitors getting there a lot quicker than that.

*Fan Brycheiniog and the Black Mountain (Mynydd Ddu) from the River Usk, near the Usk Reservoir.*

**1** Set off by continuing (SE) up the obvious broad track with the river to your right. You'll shortly cross a bridge, where a stream comes down from the left, but stay on the main track and follow it easily up with the tumbling Afon Sawdde to your right.

**2** About half way up, the way ahead is blocked by a gate that leads to the old waterworks filter beds, which are now used as fish hatcheries. Bear left, through a gap in the wall, and then turn right to follow a narrow and very rough path above the pools, keeping an eye out for jumping fish.

*Llyn y Fan Fach.*
*A great spot for kids.*

3 The path soon drops back down onto the main track and you can follow this easily upwards again, shortly crossing a bridge that leads on to the other bank of the river. Keep heading up, with the river now down to your left, and after another few minutes of easy walking, you'll arrive at a fork with a grassy path leading off to the left (SSE).

4 Both ways lead to the reservoir but for ease of way-finding, keep ahead on the main track , and a few more paces will see you arrive at the reservoir. The small hut immediately ahead of the lakes is an emergency shelter, and the towering cliffs that seem to drop almost all the way down into the water, fall from a mountain called Bannau Sir Gaer. The cliffs are often referred to as the Carmarthen Fans.

5 It is possible to forge a way right around the lake if you fancy it, but most people, having got this far, find somewhere nice to sit, and spend the next few hours soaking up the sunshine and the scenery. To return, simply retrace your steps down past the hatchery. The descent usually takes less time than the initial climb.

*Llyn y Fan Fach is what's often known as a glacial lake, one of two in this chain of mountains, as its waters are held in place by banks of debris, called moraine, which were formed by the retreating glaciers at the end of the last ice age. It is sometimes known as the 'magic lake' for the part it plays in a local legend about a lady of the lake and a local shepherd boy. The lady, beautiful beyond words, is said to have risen from the lake and the boy, whose name was Rhiwallon, fell instantly for her charms and asked her to marry him. She agreed and they wed on the one strange condition that he should never strike her with iron.*

*The lady possessed many magic skills and was able to conjure up medicinal potions from herbs and flowers, the art of which she passed on to her eldest son, also named Rhiwallon. Eventually the shepherd did strike her with iron and true to her word she left him and returned to the lake taking all their possessions with her. Rhiwallon was distraught and never got over his loss, but their son made the most of his coaching and went on to become a famous healer, in turn passing his skills on to others and giving rise to a line of local healers who became known as the Physicians of Myddfai.*

*Whilst initially sounding rather far fetched it is thought by many that the story goes back to the arrival of the Iron Age in Wales. The lady may have been from Bronze Age people living in the area which would explain her knowledge of herbal medicine and her special healing powers as well as her fear of iron. Most bizarrely, Myddfai was indeed home to a line of doctors, going back over six hundred years.*

*Bannau Sir Gaer and Llyn y Fan Fach from the west.*

# 10 Carreg Cennen

*Easy walking, stunning views and a visit to one of the most dramatic castles in the whole of Wales.*

Wales has many castles but few come close to the drama of Carreg Cennen – a semi-ruined, dragon's-den type of edifice perched upon towering cliffs at the far western tip of the Brecon Beacons National Park. It surveys foothills rather than mountains (although the Black Mountain is visible on the eastern skyline) and these foothills offer easy walking as well as fantastic views back to the castle. By starting and finishing at the castle itself, it's easy to make time for exploration – well worthwhile, especially if you take a torch – and it also affords an opportunity to enjoy lunch or a snack in the wonderful restaurant in the farm buildings nearby. It's a magical outing at any time of year but the scenery is particularly beguiling in autumn when the oak and beech woods that surround the castle are at their most colourful.

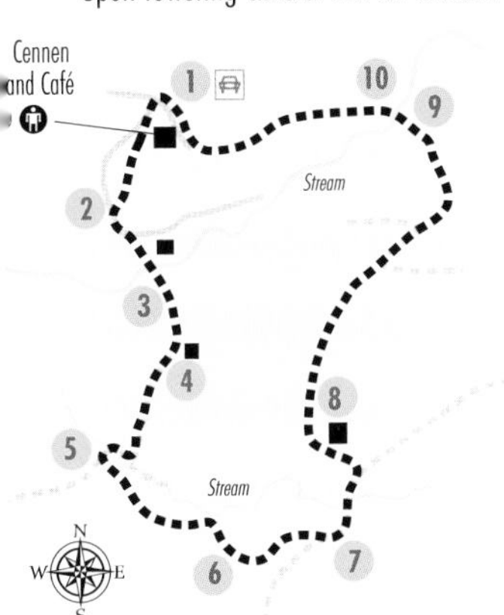


**Level:**
**Length:** 4 miles
**Terrain:** Easy to follow footpaths over pastures and meadows and through deciduous woodland. Can be muddy in places.
**Park & Start:** Carreg Cennen car park, at the end of a minor lane, a few miles east of Trapp. Signed from most directions.
**Start Ref:** SN666193 Postcode SA19 6UA
**Public Transport:** None
**Nearest Refreshments:** Restaurant in Castle Farm at the start.

1 Set off by heading from the car park towards the castle and then as you reach the farm buildings turn right to walk across a gravel area to a gate. Now head downhill across a field (SW) and head for a stile and gate in the bottom left hand corner. Note the sign which has a castle symbol on it. This will be seen throughout the walk.

2 Climb the stile and turn left onto the lane. Ignore one stile on the right and curve around to the left before taking a second stile on the right, this one is waymarked to Llwyn-bedw. Head down through the field and bear slightly right to climb another stile in a corner. Now drop steeply down to another stile, which you cross, before continuing across another field and over a footbridge that spans the Afon Cennen.

3 Bear half left to head uphill to another stile and cross this to continue steeply up, keeping parallel to a fence and line of trees. At the top, you'll reach a farm, where you should turn right (SE) onto the drive.

4 Follow this across fields and between trees to a ford. Cross the stream and bear right and then left to a waymarked footpath on the left. Take this and follow another track along (SSE) with a hedged bank on the right.

5 Cross a footbridge and continue to a stile, which you cross; and now bear slightly right along an enclosed track that emerges onto open ground before continuing alongside the infant Afon Loughor.

6 Climb a stile (the source of the river is to the right of this, over another stile) and continue as the track winds leftwards and climbs slightly, with a fence on the right. Continue around to the left to a stile and then bear right to pass between two depressions. Continue straight ahead (ENE) to another stile that leads onto a lane.

7 Turn left and follow this up to a right hand bend. Keep straight ahead here (NW) onto a track that leads between a fence and a bank. As the track curves right to the

*Carreg Cennen Castle atop steep cliffs.*

*Carreg Cennen is something of a rarity in Wales as it actually built by the Welsh rather than the Normans. The layout as seen was constructed in the 12th century although there is plenty of evidence of earlier settlements on the site. Despite its seemingly impenetrable location, the castle changed hands many times during its heyday and was eventually demolished in the 15th-century, immediately after the War of the Roses.*

Carreg Cennen Castle.

house, keep left to cross a stile and follow the waymarked path along with a fence to the left. This eventually swings right, with fences on both sides, and climbs towards the brow of a hill. Continue over the hill and down again to a stile that leads onto a sunken track.

8 Follow this down to join a broad track at hairpin bend and turn left to take the lower track. And then, as the track turns sharply left, bear right to cross a stile and drop down a stony, tree-and hedge-lined path, climbing another stile and bearing left to keep a stream to your right.

9 Turn right to cross a bridge over the stream and turn left to follow the other bank. Climb another stile and keep ahead to cross another footbridge, this one over the Afon Cennen.

**10** Turn right and then immediately left (W) to follow a good footpath steeply uphill through woodland. Continue past the castle entrance at the top and follow the path down again, passing through two kissing gates before arriving back at Castle Farm. Keep ahead to the car park.

*Carreg Cennen from a distance.*

*Tree on the Black Mountain. Near Carreg Cennen Castle.*